Crabapples

How a Book is Published

Bobbie Kalman

Crabtree Publishing Company

Crabapples

created by Bobbie Kalman

For the best editorial team ever

above: Niki Walker, Greg Nickles, Tammy Everts, (Bobbie), Petrina Gentile, Lynda Hale, David Schimpky

Editor-in-Chief
Bobbie Kalman

Managing editor
Lynda Hale

Editors
Niki Walker
Petrina Gentile
Tammy Everts
Greg Nickles

Computer design
Lynda Hale

Color separations & film
Dot 'n Line Image Inc.

Printer
Worzalla Publishing Co.

Crabtree Publishing Company

350 Fifth Avenue
Suite 3308
New York
N.Y. 10118

360 York Road, RR 4,
Niagara-on-the-Lake,
Ontario, Canada
L0S 1J0

73 Lime Walk
Headington
Oxford OX3 7AD
United Kingdom

Cataloging in Publication Data
Kalman, Bobbie, 1947-
   How a book is published

(Crabapples)
Includes index.

ISBN 0-86505-618-8 (library bound)   ISBN 0-86505-718-4 (pbk.)
This book discusses the steps in publishing a book, covering
research, writing, editing, illustration, design, and printing.

1. Books - Juvenile literature. 2. Publishers and publishing -
Juvenile literature. I. Title. II. Series: Kalman, Bobbie, 1947-
Crabapples.

Z278.K3 1995   j070.5   LC 95-39851
                                                         CIP

What is in this book?

Are you an author?

Does your school have a publishing program? Many schools do. Children write books, and their teachers or classmates **edit** them. The books are then written neatly or typed by the student or teacher. After covers are put on, the books become part of a special library, ready to be enjoyed by other students.

Have you ever wondered how books are
written and published at a publishing
company? Turn the pages and find out!

Meet an author

Bobbie Kalman is an author. She has written more than 100 books. Bobbie thinks of ideas and creates books for children. She also visits schools and talks to children about the books she has written. Bobbie was a teacher years ago, and now she teaches through her books.

Most of Bobbie's books are **non-fiction**. Non-fiction books contain information about many different subjects. For example, this book gives you information about how a book is written and published.

Bobbie is a **publisher** as well as an author. A publisher decides which books will be brought out each year. Besides creating books, publishing companies also advertise and sell them.

Before deciding to publish a book, these questions need to be answered:

- Are there other books on this subject?
- How will this book be different?
- Who will read this book?
- Who will buy this book?
- How much will the book cost to publish?

Writers research and write the **manuscript**.

Teamwork

Many people work together to publish a book. They do not all work at the publishing company. The writing team researches and writes. Editors correct errors. Graphic designers make the book look good. Printers print the book. Writing and publishing books takes teamwork!

The writing team also views hundreds of slides for each book.

Graphic designers make the book look attractive.

Artists and photographers provide the pictures.

Editors read the manuscript many times to find and correct errors.

Printers use film to create pages for the printed book.

The managing editor follows her notes when directing photo shoots.

9

Brainstorming

Brainstorming is the first step in the writing process. Brainstorming means sharing ideas. Bobbie brainstorms with teachers and librarians. She visits schools to learn what kind of books children like.

Bobbie brainstorms with her editorial team about the information that should go into each book. Great ideas come from brainstorming!

The writing team discusses ideas and comes up with an **outline**. An outline keeps facts in the right order. It provides the skeleton for the body of the book. Hurray for outlines!

Using this book, find these important features:
- cover (Is it hard or soft?)
- title page
- dedication
- cataloging information
- table of contents
- copyright date
- acknowledgments
- glossary
- index
- endpapers
- author's age

Get the facts!

After writing an outline, the next step is researching. You can get information from books, encyclopedias, and magazines. You can also find the facts you need on computers, video tapes, and television programs. These research sources are called **secondary sources** of information.

As well as using secondary sources, the writing team looks for **primary sources** of information to find original facts about a topic. The team travels all over the world to interview people or observe animals in their natural environment. They "dive right in" to learn about the sea creatures that live in a coral reef.

Writing and rewriting

Bobbie and her team write manuscripts two pages at a time. Two pages that face each other are called a **spread**. The writer makes an outline of the main topics on each spread. The subheadings that tell what each paragraph is about come from this outline.

Most authors **rewrite** a manuscript many times. They add new information, switch the order of the paragraphs, make the manuscript easier to read, or change the topics in the book.

photograph

photograph

artwork

chapter heading

body text

subheading

captions

Here are some writing tips to get you started:

① Decide on the purpose of your writing.

② Read, observe, and brainstorm to come up with ideas.

③ Organize your ideas into an interesting and easy-to-follow outline.

④ Using your outline as a guide, expand on your ideas. Make your message clear.

⑤ You have just written your first draft! Read it out loud. Will your readers understand your ideas? Is your book what you wanted it to be? Until your answer is "yes," rewrite it again and again!

Editing

After a book has been rewritten many times, it is ready to be edited and proofread. Do you know the editing symbols shown on the opposite page? There are many more! You can find them in a dictionary or in a book about editing. Teach them to your friends to make editing easier and more fun!

The editing process

Editing for meaning

Editing means making changes. Editors use special marks to show what changes should be made. They make sure that the information is clear, and the language is not too difficult for children to understand.

Group editing

Each editor in the group takes a turn reading the manuscript out loud. Does it sound good? Are some words repeated too often? Reading out loud is a good way to find mistakes and share ideas.

Copy-editing and proofreading

When the editors agree that the manuscript is good, it is ready to be **copy-edited**. They look for errors in spelling and punctuation. They **proofread** the manuscript again and again to correct possible errors.

The last details

The editors must wait to write the glossary, index, and acknowledgments. The manuscript must be completed before these parts of the book can be written.

Editing marks

~~many~~	delete from the text
⊙	insert a period
∿	switch items around
t̲	change to upper case
F̸	change to lower case
/than we do	insert new text
¶	begin new paragraph
eyes bf	use boldface type

Insects have large compound eyes. Compound eyes have many tiny parts called Facets. Simple eyes only have one facet. Humans have simple eyes Insects see differently. Each facet in their/than we do eyes works separately. the insect sees ~~many~~ hundreds of pictures of the same thing.

The pictures

Most children's books have artwork or photographs to help explain the written information. Bobbie uses both. She and her team look at each spread and decide what kinds of pictures are needed. Artists and photographers work on the pictures while the manuscript is being edited.

The writers discuss their ideas with an artist, who then draws a rough sketch. When the sketch is approved, the artist completes the final picture.

Finding photographs for a book is called **photo research**. The editors call photographers on the telephone and ask them to send pictures for a book. They view hundreds of slides and photographs but choose only 30 to 50 for each book. The editors look for sharp, colorful, and exciting pictures.

Photo shoots

A ballerina concentrates on her moves as she practices at the **barre** in *Ballet School.*

When the editors cannot find the photographs they need, they hire photographers to take pictures for a book. Sometimes Bobbie takes the pictures. Taking pictures at a special place is called "doing a **photo shoot**." Photo shoots are hard work, but they are fun!

This Spanish web performance was photographed for *Circus Fun.*

A model is fitted into a tight corset in *Children's Clothing of the 1800s.*

Bobbie and Nicola take time out for a hug during a shoot for *Nicola's Floating Home*.

Marc Crabtree has taken pictures for several of Bobbie's books, including three books on Vietnam.

Bobbie took this cover picture during a fiesta in Mexico.

These two young pioneers are the main characters in *A Child's Day*.

Designing the book

Once the photographs have been selected, Lynda, the graphic designer, and Bobbie design the book. They put the photographs and artwork together with the text to make the book look good. Designing is like working on a jigsaw puzzle—everything has to fit just right!

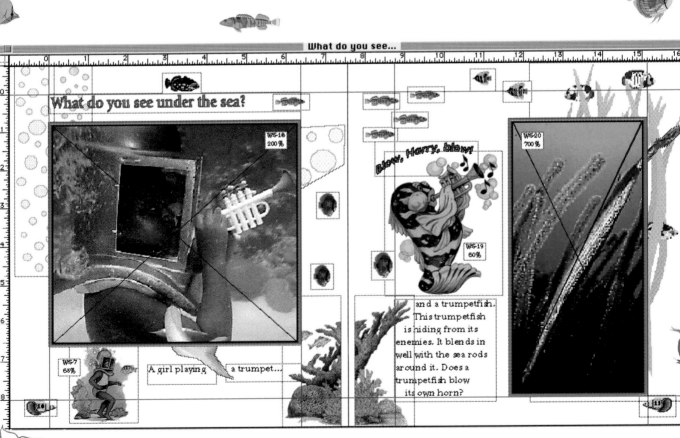

The book is designed on a computer. Using a special computer program, Lynda arranges, or **lays out**, each spread. Petrina puts the pictures into the **scanner**. The pictures are then **sized** to fit on the page. The entire book is stored on a computer disk, which is sent to the **film house**.

Easter hunt

Help Edward find his Easter eggs. Ben the Easter Bunny has put them in some very unusual places! Can you spot all 35 eggs hidden in the picture below? You may have to turn the book upside down or stand on your head to find some of them!

Separating the colors

Look at the illustration above. Make a list of the colors you see. All the colors that you have named come from the **primary colors**—red (magenta), blue (cyan), and yellow. Black makes the pictures look sharper. The text is also black.

The film house makes four pieces of film—one each of cyan, magenta, yellow, and black. The four pictures on this page show how the spread on the opposite page has been separated into these colors.

Page proofs are made from the four layers of film. The editors check the proofs for dirt spots and scratches. They proofread the manuscript again.

The editors check the colors of the pictures. Sometimes the colors on the proofs are very different from the colors in the photographs or artwork.

The film separators can change the way a picture looks. They can make it brighter by taking away some cyan and adding more yellow. They can sharpen it with black.

In print

After the film is made, the book is ready to be printed. The printer makes metal **plates** from the four pieces of film— one for each color. The plates are put on a big **printing press**. Each plate presses either cyan, magenta, yellow, or black ink onto paper. The inks blend to create all the colors you see.

The book is printed on one big sheet of paper. After the first side is dry, the other side is printed. Lynda checks the printed page for dirt spots. She makes sure that the colors match the colors in the proofs.

The printed sheets are cut, **collated**, folded, glued, and sewn together. They are **bound** with hard or soft covers.

Advice to young authors

Bobbie Kalman's books are very popular with children because of one magic ingredient—Bobbie and her writing team "live" their books. Whether it is researching clothing of the past or studying rainforest birds, the team gets totally involved.

Here are some practical ideas to make your book fun to write:

- write about subjects that interest you
- do as much primary research as possible
- get involved in an event and write about your experiences
- illustrate your book with photographs or drawings
- share your writing with others— put it on a bulletin board or read it out loud

Students in the photograph above put on a circus show and then wrote stories about how it feels to be part of a circus. When you put your feelings and opinions into a story or book, people will enjoy reading your creation. Your writing will be special if your love shines through!

Words to know

author A person who writes books

barre A wooden bar that helps dancers keep their balance

bind To fasten or enclose pages between covers

brainstorm To share creative ideas

collate To assemble pages in their proper order

copy-edit To look for small errors in spelling, punctuation, or spacing

edit To correct and prepare a piece of writing for publication

film house A place where a book is put onto film to be used later in printing

lay out To arrange the text and pictures used in a book

manuscript A piece of writing that has not yet been published

non-fiction Describes a piece of writing that is based on facts

outline A framework on which a piece of writing is built

page proof A sample page that is checked and corrected before the book is printed

photo research The act of looking for photographs to publish

photo shoot The act of taking pictures for a book, magazine, or newspaper

plate A metal sheet used in printing

primary colors The basic colors of red, blue, and yellow from which all other colors are made

primary source A firsthand source of information, such as a trip to a place or an event

printing press A machine used to print books, magazines, and newspapers

proofread To read a manuscript and check for errors

publisher A person who produces and sells writing for others to read

rewrite To improve a piece of writing by writing it again

scanner A device that changes artwork or photographs into computerized images for use in book design

secondary source A second-hand source of information, such as a book, newspaper article, or encyclopedia

size To adjust artwork or a photo so that it fits into the page design

spread Two facing pages in a book

text The words in a piece of writing

Index

Acknowledgments

Special thanks to Taylor Newman, Nicola Hill, Peta-Gay Ramos, Michael Alfonsi, Sarah Pallek, Victoria Chuop, Danielle Gentile, David Cox, Jacqui Tracy, Peter Crabtree, Marc Crabtree, Andrea Crabtree, Samantha Crabtree, Caroline Crabtree, Kelly Ferguson, Vrajaprana, Natalie Bullard, Janine Schaub, Antoinette DeBiasi, Worzalla Publishing Company, The National Ballet School, Peggy Wohlfarth and the students of Mechanicsburg Area Schools, the students of Eggert Road Elementary School, Carol Harder and the students of Virgil Public School, Leigh Adamson, Brian Adamson, Rose Marie Cipryk, Oliver Nguyen, and Samantha Green

Photographs

All photographs are the property of Crabtree Publishing Company and were taken by the editorial team except the following:

Chris Collins: cover, pages 5, 8 (bottom left), 11, 16, 19 (bottom)

Marc Crabtree: pages 20 (top), 21 (bottom right)

Peter Crabtree: pages 7, 8 (top), 10 (bottom), 19 (top), 21 (top left), 28 (top)

Christopher Hartley: page 13 (bottom)

Jacqui Tracy: page 10 (top)

Illustrations

Barb Bedell: pages 18, 22

Maureen Shaughnessy: page 24

About the author

Bobbie Kalman was born in Hungary and speaks English, Hungarian, French, and German. She has traveled and lived in different countries, including Nassau, Bahamas, where she taught years ago.

Bobbie has recently worked on four books in the Bahamas. One of them was photographed under the sea and another on a sailboat. "Working in other countries is always lots of fun. I love being a writer because every day is different and challenging," says Bobbie.

While in Nassau, Bobbie dresses Bahamian-style.

Bobbie's family: Peter Crabtree, Marc, Andrea, Samantha, and Caroline, standing with Bobbie

Bobbie has fun with a child in a Nassau school.

1 2 3 4 5 6 7 8 9 0 Printed in the U.S.A. 4 3 2 1 0 9 8 7 6 5

Run to the Rainbow

Modern Curriculum Press
BEGINNING
TO
READ
Series

Library of Congress Cataloging in Publication Data

Hillert, Margaret.
  Run to the rainbow.

  SUMMARY: Three children, searching for the rainbow, see many colorful objects.
  [1. Rainbow—Fiction]   I. Corey, Barbara.   II. Title.
PZ7.H558Ru   [E]   79-23889
ISBN 0-8136-5065-8 Hardbound
ISBN 0-8136-5565-X Paperback

Library of Congress Catalog Card Number: 79-23889

20 19   06 05 04 03 02 01 00

Run to the Rainbow

Margaret Hillert

Illustrated by Barbara Corey

4

Oh, look.
Look at that.
Do you see what I see?
Look at it.

Look up, up, up.
Look way up.
How pretty it is!

6

I see something red.
I see yellow.
I see blue.
I like this.

Look where it goes.
We can go, too.
We can find out where
it goes.
We can run and find it.

Come on now.
Out, out, out.
Go, go, go.
This is the way.

One, two, three.
Here we go.
Run, run, run.
This is fun.

12

I see it.
I see it.
Look at that.
Do you see that?
Come on.
Oh, come on.

Oh, no!
That is not it.
See what it is.
That is not it.

I guess we will have
to go on.
We will look, look, look.
Now what is that?
What do you see?

This looks good.
It is pretty.
Mother likes it, but
it is not what we want.

Come on. Come on.
Run, run, run.
I see something.
Something looks like it.

Is this it?

Is this it down here?

No, I guess not.

Not this. Not this.

Cars make this.

21

Here we go.
Away, away.
We will find it.
See that. See that.

Oh, this looks like it,
but it is not the big one
It is a little one.

And I can make a little
one, too.
Look what I can do.
Do you like this little one?

Now where can we go?
What is that?
I see something.
Run, run, run.

27

Oh, look here.
Look here.
Something for us to eat.
Something good, good, good.

We did not find it.

We did not find the big one.

I guess we can not
go where it is.

Here it is.
Oh, here it is.
Come, look here.

No, this is not it,
but it looks like it.
It is pretty,
and it is here where we are.
This is good.

Margaret Hillert, author and poet, has written many books for young readers. She is a former first-grade teacher and lives in Birmingham, Michigan.

Run to the Rainbow uses the 62 words listed below.

a	find	make	that
and	for	mother	the
are	fun		this
at		no	three
away	go	not	to
	goes	now	too
big	good		two
blue	guess	oh	
but		on	up
	have	one	us
can	here	out	
come	how		want
cars		pretty	way
	I		we
did	is	red	what
do	it	run	where
down			will
	like	see	
eat	little	something	yellow
	look(s)		you